fabric
Dyeing
for beginners

Vimala
McClure

American Quilter's Society
P. O. Box 3290 • Paducah, KY 42002-3290
www.AQSquilt.com

Located in Paducah, Kentucky, the American Quilter's Society (AQS) is dedicated to promoting the accomplishments of today's quilters. Through its publications and events, AQS strives to honor today's quiltmakers and their work and to inspire future creativity and innovation in quiltmaking.

EDITOR: BARBARA SMITH
GRAPHIC DESIGN: AMY CHASE
COVER DESIGN: MICHAEL BUCKINGHAM
PHOTOGRAPHY: CHARLES R. LYNCH
HOW-TO PHOTOGRAPHY: VIMALA MCCLURE
PHOTOGRAPHY MODEL: BARBARA FREY

Library of Congress Cataloging-in-Publication Data
McClure, Vimala Schneider, 1952-
        Fabric dyeing for beginners / by Vimala McClure
                        p.   cm.
        ISBN 1-57432-813-1
        1. Dyes and dyeing, domestic. 2. Dyes and dyeing--Textile fibers.
        I. American Quilter's Society. II. Title.
TT853.M38   2003
746.667'.3--dc21   02-154329

Additional copies of this book may be ordered from the American Quilter's Society, PO Box 3290, Paducah, KY 42002-3290, or online at www.AQSquilt.com.

Fabric dyeing can be hazardous to your health. Be sure to carefully read and follow the packaging directions for handling the chemicals used in your projects. You can contact the manufacturer or supplier if you have any questions concerning the safety of dye chemicals. AQS disclaims all warranties both express and implied concerning the use of the published information.

Dedication

To my friends, enthusiastic supporters,
and Luana and Paul Rubin of eQuilter.com,
whose generosity and kindness know no bounds.

Acknowledgments

I would like to thank the members of the Quilt Mavericks, an online guild, for selflessly donating examples of blocks and quilts for this book; and Caryl Bryer Fallert for her support, help, and encouragement. Her workshops and quilts took me to a whole new level of quiltmaking, which sparked my interest in dyeing fabrics. A special thanks goes to Barbara Frey for being my photography model.

Contents

pickle-jar fabrics

TURTLE MOON, 36" x 32", Wildlife Series, by the author. The turtle's claws are shells. Fabrics: pickle-dyed pieces in the stained-glass border, strip-pieced water, and moon.

INTRODUCTION

Perhaps you have admired hand-dyed fabrics, with their luscious watercolor washes and tie-dyed patterns, perfect for creating skies, water, or stained glass and for achieving light effects in your quilts. I lusted after these hand-dyed gems at trade shows but shrank from the cost. On the other hand, the complicated instructions for dyeing fabric myself were daunting.

In 1992, I began to experiment with various methods of dyeing fabric, eager to have available as generous a palette of colors and textures as possible. Then I discovered several methods that allowed me to create my own unique fabrics with ease, for about one tenth the cost. While taking the last jar of homemade blueberry preserves from my pantry, I paused to hold the jar up to the sunlight and admire the beautiful color. I suddenly thought, what if the jar could be used to dye my fabric? If I could pack the fabric in the jar and "pickle" it, I would need a lot less space, and a cookbook approach might help me understand the whole process more clearly.

I imagined this process would be difficult or time-consuming, but in enumerating the steps and listing the materials needed, I found, to my delight, that this way of dyeing small pieces was much easier than I had thought. Having finished putting up my fruit, I knew I would never use the canning items again, so most of the tools for dyeing were already on hand. The spoons, cups, jars, etc., needed only a thorough cleaning. I changed the title of the trunk in which these supplies were stored to "Dye Tools" instead of "Pickling Items," so there was a single place for everything and no doubt as to which items were reserved for dyeing.

> Just as I never used my pickling items, measuring cups, spoons, etc., for anything else, I would never use my dyeing items for anything but dye projects. Of course, they are always kept well out of reach of children.

Using a color wheel given to me by Caryl Bryer Fallert and notes from past dyeing experiments, I made my own recipe. With great anticipation, I followed that recipe and it worked! A whole color wheel of fabulous mottled textures was created, rich colors in several gradations and combinations. Referring to my color wheel and its accompanying recipe, I can easily mix up small batches of exactly what I need.

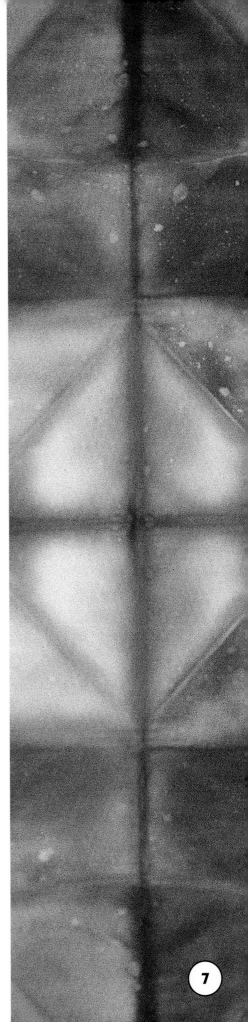

I have continued to use these methods for my own quilts and have developed procedures for those types of dyeing that are difficult for me to understand and do. I need a method that can be broken down into steps to be done on separate days. Parents of small children also need dye methods that are easy to do and can be separated into small steps over weeks or even months. In addition, they need methods that are not messy, are easy to clean up, and do not leave dye containers where curious children can get into them.

In my quilts, I want some different fabrics that direct the eye around the quilt and provide some patterning that is different from anything I can find. The idea of folding fabric and dyeing it occurred to me, so I tried it and found I loved the fabrics. They provide beautiful luminous color, and the lines created by the dye collected in the folds can be used in quilt design. In addition, quilting over the fold lines of a fold-dyed fabric makes it look as if all these elements had been pieced.

I had experimented with tie-dye before, making tee shirts for my kids. Tie-dyeing produces sunbursts, spirals, and circular designs that add further interest to parts of my quilts. Small pieces of these fabrics add amazing stripes and curves to pieced elements, which can be done in any size. I had seen Japanese Shibori-type dyed fabrics, with magical lines of light moving through them. Again, I developed an easy method for achieving similar effects in my fabrics.

Chapter One presents some basic information, including safety precautions. In Chapter Two, you will find how to make both a 12- and a 24-gradation color wheel of pickled fabrics. The basic terms and tools of these methods are also outlined, and the recipes for the basic elements of each dye batch are given. Fat quarters and small pieces are dyed in half-pint jelly (or pickle) jars. For larger pieces, the recipes must be doubled and the jar size increased.

Chapter Three shows how to make fold-dyed fabrics by using similar methods to those in Chapter Two, but folded fabrics produce a geometric pattern as opposed to the crinkled look of pickled fabrics. These fabrics are dyed in zipper-locked plastic bags. You can also fold-dye your pickled fabrics to add another dimension to the fabric patterning, if you like.

Chapter Four presents several ways to achieve different patterns of traditional tie-dyed fabrics. These fabrics are made by using a flat waterproof surface, small wooden dowels, twine, and zipper-locked plastic bags. Also in Chapter Four, a simple method for achieving the look of Shibori or Japanese-style tie dye is presented. The fabrics are dyed by using PVC pipe, twine, and zipper-locked plastic bags.

Another method, described in Chapter Five, involves stenciling forms over the top of hand-dyed fabrics. In this way, you can add another layer of image and illusion to the quilt. I like to use shapes, such as leaves, butterflies, and abstract designs. I will show you how to make a thick paint from the dye solution and how to cut stencils and apply the paint over previously dyed fabric to achieve airbrushed-like effects, such as floating leaves, butterflies, and geometric objects like circles and triangles.

Each method is illustrated, and examples of fabric swatches and quilt blocks are displayed. We will start with some tips that will help your work go more smoothly and provide you with a summary of safety rules, and a glossary of terms used throughout the book. A resources section on page 79 will give you the names and addresses of suppliers for the materials you will need for each chapter.

I encourage you to experiment and find your own ways of creating new and interesting patterning in your dyed fabrics. You'll find that many of your favorite pieces come from "thinking outside the box" – experimenting with your own techniques that turn out to be great additions to your repertoire.

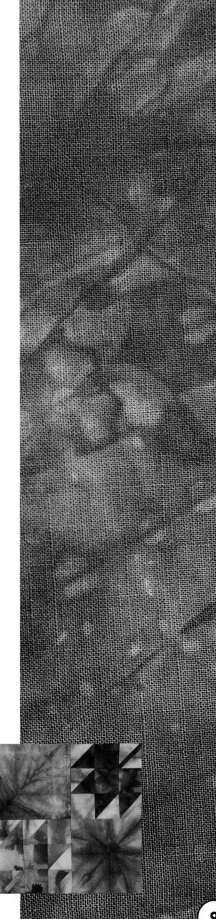

tie-dyed fabrics

Tied-dyed stars

"DANCING STARS", by Becky Wall, Wilmington, Delaware.

chapter 1

General Instructions

I dye my fabrics in a spontaneous way. After learning the basic measurements and how the chemicals work together from dye manufacturer's pamphlets and my own experimentation, I used that knowledge to simplify my approach so it was more suited to my way of doing things. I developed a way of working that is unique to my own needs but which is also great for beginners who want to experiment with dyeing fabric without committing to the kind of surface design covered in more advanced texts. If you want precise measurements that produce exact outcomes, ratios of dye to fabric weight, and so on, a more advanced book may assist you.

Basic Equipment and Supplies

This list will give you a general idea of the types of equipment and supplies you will need for fabric dyeing. In each chapter, you will find an additional specific for the dye process described in that chapter.

- Mixing box (See How to Make a Mixing Box, page 16.)
- Dust mask (Industrial or paper masks are available from hard ware stores, catalogs, or dye manufacturers.)
- Rubber gloves (Look for doctor-style gloves in bulk. They are thin so you can feel what you are doing.)
- Apron or clothes designated for dyeing
- Mercerized cotton or prepared for dyeing (PFD) fabric
- Tubs and containers
- Measuring cups
- Measuring spoons
- Chopsticks or other stirrers
- Jars (Size depends on fabric size.)
- Zipper-locked plastic bags
- Paper towels
- Drop cloths or newspapers
- Procion MX® dyes: yellow, blue, and red
- Dye activator solution (page 16)
- Chem water (page 16) (water, salt, urea, water softener)
- Synthrapol soap
- Print Paste Mix® (for painting techniques only)

general instructions

Safety

The dyes we use for these methods are Procion MX fiber-reactive dyes. These dyes are extremely toxic, and it is important that you follow all the safety measures. Dyes should never be handled without a dust mask and gloves (Figure 1). Never eat or drink anything while dyeing. Do not use any dye

Figure 1. *You can use either an industrial type dust mask or a paper one.*

tool or jar for food. Be sure you cover yourself well with an apron or special clothing you use only for dyeing. Always prepare dyes inside a mixing box. Handle dyes in an area where there is plenty of ventilation.

Definitions

Chem water. A solution of water, salt, urea, water softener, and a tiny bit of Synthrapol soap to which powdered dyes are added. After adding dye, the combination of the urea with the dye powder creates a chemical reaction, and over time, the color will become weaker. *Storage:* Chem water can be kept indefinitely *before* adding dye. It may be stored with dye powder mixed in indefinitely if kept in a cool place and not mixed with dye activator solution. The strength of the activated dye color will get weaker as time goes by.

Dye. Powdered dye from a dye supplier, such as Dharma Trading Company or Pro-Chem (see Resources, page 79). Ask your supplier for a sample sheet of available colors of dye powder. Dye powder is extremely toxic. Do not open a jar of powdered dye without wearing a mask over your nose and mouth, rubber or plastic gloves on your hands, and working in a mixing box. *Storage:* The powder can be stored almost indefinitely in a cool, dark place.

Dye activator solution. A mixture of dye activator (sodium carbonate and soda ash fixer) and warm water used to soak your fabric before applying dye solution. The soda ash is a mild alkali that bonds the dye to the cellulose fibers of the fabric. The soda ash should be dissolved in hot water, then the solution should be used at a warm

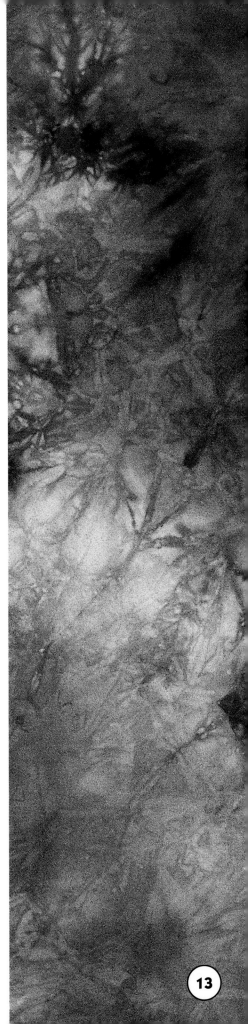

temperature. When combined with dye solution, the activator will react fast. It needs about an hour or so to react almost completely, but if you can leave the fabric in it for a longer time, you will achieve the maximum depth of color. *Storage:* Dye activator or soda ash fixer is a white powder that can be stored indefinitely in powdered form. The solution can also be stored indefinitely and reused many times.

Dye solution. A mixture of powdered dye and chem water. This solution is poured into jelly jars or applied to pre-soaked fabric. *Storage:* It may be stored up to a week in a cool, dark place. After that, the color gradually loses intensity. Refrigerated, the dye solution, not mixed with dye activator solution, will keep for another week, but it must be brought to room temperature before being used to dye fabric.

Heat set. Some applications of dye need to be heat set. Cover the area to be set with a pressing cloth or brown paper. Press with a hot, dry iron for 10 seconds, then cool. Repeat twice more. Heat setting is only required for the painting methods described in Chapter Five, page 61.

Mercerized fabric. Fabric treated during manufacture with caustic soda. The treatment gives fabric luster and strength and makes it receptive to dyes. Mercerized fabric dyes 25 percent darker than other fabrics. I recommend using a mercerized cotton with a thread count of 200 or higher. Mercerized cotton takes Procion MX dyes beautifully. This fabric is more expensive than cotton-print cloth, but the quality is well worth the extra cost for the serious fabric artist. Note that a mercerized fabric with a high thread count is more difficult to hand quilt.

PFD fabric. Fabric that has been prepared for dyeing. This 100 percent cotton fabric has been "scoured" to remove any finishes that would prevent dye from completely bonding with the fabric (see Resources, page 79).

Print Paste Mix®. A powder of sodium alginate (seaweed) is mixed with urea to thicken dye for painting. The mixture retards the flow of the dye solution for special applications, such as stenciling or stamping. *Storage:* Print Paste Mix can be stored indefinitely in either dry or mixed form.

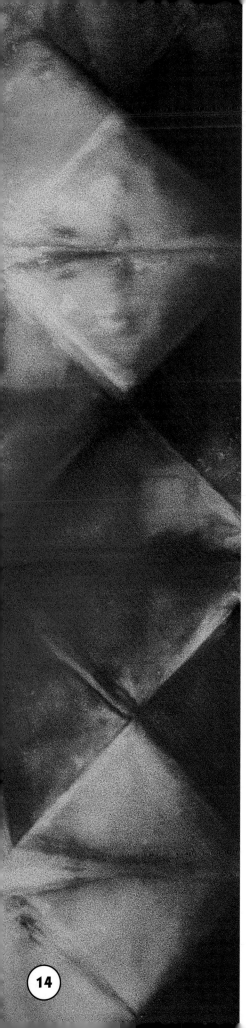

Print paste solution. A viscous liquid made by adding Print Paste Mix to hot water. It is best to mix the print paste solution at least the day before using it, to obtain the right consistency. Print paste solution can be thinned by adding hot water. This ingredient will only be used in small amounts.

Salt. Adding salt helps to deepen and intensify colors. You can use any commercial salt, including iodized salt, from the grocery store. Add salt as indicated in How to Make Chem Water, page 16.

Synthrapol® soap. This liquid soap serves three purposes: 1. It scrubs out any finishes or impurities that may interfere with dyeing. Pre-wash your fabric with hot water and ¼ cup Synthrapol per small load. This step is not necessary for PFD fabric.

2. It is used to wash fabric after dyeing. It suspends the excess dye in water and washes it away so there is no bleeding between fabrics and no dye residue in your washing machine. With Synthrapol, you can wash all the color-wheel fabrics at once, and each will come out crystal clear.

3. Add a few drops to the dye solution to prevent clumping of powdered dyes. *Storage:* Synthrapol can be stored indefinitely.

Urea granules. Also called organic nitrogen, urea is used in the dye solution to draw moisture and keep fabric damp longer during the curing process for deeper, more intense color. Use ¾ cup of urea granules per quart of hot water. When dissolving urea, use hot water, then allow the solution to cool to a warm temperature before mixing anything else with it. *Storage:* Urea granules are tiny, white round balls that can be stored indefinitely.

Water softener. Especially in areas where tap water is hard, that is, containing minerals that can prevent the dye from being thoroughly absorbed into and bonded with the fabric, adding water softener to the dye solution helps the fabric to absorb the dye. The water softener neutralizes metal salts, allowing your solutions to work as well as possible. Any commercial water softener from the grocery store will do. The addition of water softener may make the chem water look blue, but the blue color will not affect your dye colors.

Dyeing Tips

The following suggestions will provide the beginner with a practical approach to dyeing fabrics:

• Make the pickled fabrics (page 19) first before moving on to experiment with the other methods. Pickling will give you a solid foundation for the steps involved and make you comfortable with the dyeing process. All of the terms and recipes are explained, so you can refer to this chapter whenever you need to.

• I suggest that you get more than the minimum amount of each chemical listed on page 11, except soda ash fixer. This way, you will have enough to experiment with all the methods and enough in case you need to start over when mixing a solution.

• Dye light, medium, and dark batches on separate days. If you have little time or need to conserve energy, you can schedule steps one and two, three through five, and six through eight on separate days (see How to Pickle Fabrics, page 22).

• Each yard of fabric will make four fat quarters (approximately 18" x 20"). For some of the processes, such as those in Chapters Three and Five, you may want to use square pieces. I suggest 18" x 18", but you can use whatever size you like. The remaining fabric can be dyed by using any of the methods in Chapters One through Five. In Chapter Two, you can dye approximately six yards of fabric. You will have dye activator solution left over for the methods in the other chapters.

• Fabrics can be over-dyed. For example, if you have light colors and need darker ones, or if you would like to experiment with fold-dyed methods by using fabrics you have pickle dyed, feel free to do so. It is effective to make pickled fabrics, then over-dye them with one or more of the other processes. For example, you can use the fold-dyed method over a pickle-dyed fabric. You can then stencil forms over that by using the methods in Chapter Five, page 61.

• These dyes should be used with lukewarm water. You can use hot water in the final wash to scour away any dye residue. A hot water wash will not remove the dye because it is bonded to the fabric. You can also use hot water to mix the dye activator solution and chem water, but this should be cooled to warm before adding dye.

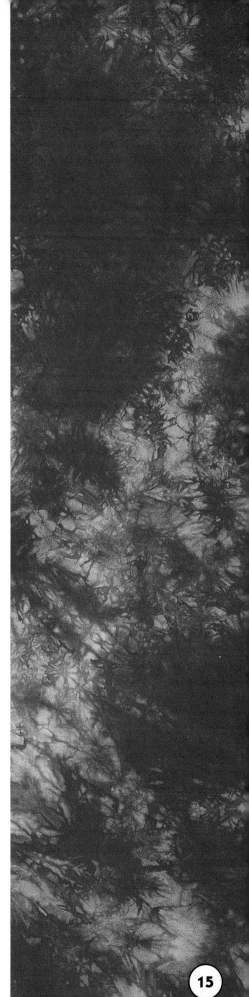

general instructions

• You can reuse dye activator solution. Each time you use it, you may need to add appropriate amounts of hot water and dye activator (soda ash fixer) to warm up the solution. It needs to be warm, about 90 degrees, to work best. If you have leftover dye activator solution that has become cold, add a gallon of hot water and ¾ cup dye activator powder to warm it up. If it still seems cold to you, repeat.

• Procion MX fiber-reactive dyes bond with the fabric at the molecular level, so they are true to color, wash-fast, and more lightfast than dyes in most commercial fabrics.

How to Make a Mixing Box

It is best to mix your dyes in a mixing box so tiny particles of powdered dye do not circulate in the air. To make a mixing box, cut the flaps off a cardboard box. Cut a U-shaped hole in one side, big enough to comfortably fit both hands. Line the bottom of box, so when it is inverted, wet newspapers will be on top to catch floating particles. Then place the box over the jar of chem water and stir the dye powder into the chem water (Figure 2).

Figure 2. *Make a mixing box for handling dye powder safely.*

How to Make Dye Activator

In a large, shallow plastic tub, mix 3 gallons warm water with 1½ cups dye activator powder. Cover the mixture with a lid.

How to Make Chem Water

Fill a plastic, wide-mouth gallon jug three-fourths full with hot water and add 3 cups urea granules, 3 Tablespoons table salt, and 4 teaspoons water softener. Stir thoroughly to dissolve. To mix the three base colors, page 17, start by filling three quart-sized containers a little more than three-fourths full with chem water. Add a couple of drops of Synthrapol soap to each jar. Mix thoroughly. For other colors, the same recipe applies.

general instructions

How to Make Dye Solution

Assemble stirrers, measuring spoons, dyes, and chem water. (Be sure to wear your mask, gloves, and apron.) Mix the dye powder inside the mixing box you have made to prevent dye particles from circulating in the air. Add yellow, blue, and red dye powder to respective quart containers as follows:

Three Base Colors

Choose whether you want dark, medium, or light dyes, then make a jar of each base color in that value. The amounts listed are per quart of chem water. They are approximate and apply to any shade of red, yellow, and blue, including lemon (cool yellow), fuchsia (cool red), and turquoise blue.

Yellow	Blue	Red
Light: 2 teaspoons	Light: 1 teaspoon	Light: ½ teaspoon
Medium: 5 teaspoons	Medium: 3 teaspoons	Medium 2 teaspoons
Dark: 8 teaspoons	Dark: 5 teaspoons	Dark: 3 teaspoon

Other colors may require different amounts of dye powder. You may want to use other colors straight from the manufacturer, who will usually send you a color chart of all their Procion MX fiber-reactive dyes.

Pamphlets from the dye manufacturer can tell you exactly what ratio of dye to chem water will be needed for each color. Because there are so many available colors (literally hundreds!), I use the same measurements as given previously for the yellow dye to create light, medium, and dark batches of other colors. This is because a quart of chem water cannot contain any more than 8 teaspoons of dye in solution, so it is unnecessary to ever go over that amount. For example, if I have a dye powder called Forest Green, to make a light batch, I would use 2 teaspoons dye powder; for a medium batch, 5 teaspoons; and for a dark batch, 8 teaspoons. This is a rough guide. You can experiment with various colors to find the amount you need for the depth of color you want.

pickle-jar fabrics

Pickle-dyed dark blue, fold-dyed light blue
Nine Patch block by Wendy J. Crawford, Beavercreek, Oregon.

chapter 2

Pickle-Jar Fabrics

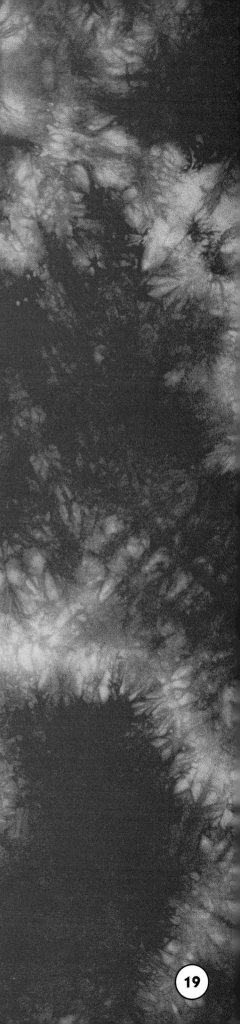

Pickle-jar fabrics are a treasured addition to any quiltmaker's palette. They will add light and movement to your quilt in a way no other type of commercial fabric can. The basic recipe is presented here. I suggest you make an abundance of these fabrics in many colors to mix in with the commercial cottons in your quilts. When a pattern calls for a solid color, consider using a pickle-jar fabric instead.

> Because dyes are toxic, items that could accidentally be used with food, such as measuring spoons and cups, need to be marked as dye utensils and stored with your dye equipment.

Additional Supplies (see also page 11)

- Fabric: six yards PFD fabric for each 24-step batch
- One gallon container with pour spout
- Three quart containers. Pour spouts are helpful.
- One dozen half-pint pickle or jelly jars with lids, for 12-step color wheel, or two dozen for a 24-step color wheel
  If you've bought new jars, keep the boxes with the jar separators. Cut off box flaps.
- Two or three plastic tubs for transporting fabrics
- Two-cup measuring cups with pour spouts
- Large shallow plastic tub (with a cover) that will hold at least three gallons of liquid
- Three cups urea granules. Get a larger amount if required by supplier.
- Eight ounces each of Procion MX dyes
  Three Base Colors:
  red MX8B (fuchsia)
  yellow MX8G
  turquoise MXG
- One pint Synthrapol soap
- Three cups dye activator or soda ash fixer
  Get the smallest amount of whatever you are required to order, as long as you have at least three cups.

pickle-jar fabrics

Dye Colors

You can select any pure red, yellow, and blue dyes you like. The colors listed in the table on page 17 will give you cool bright hues, while other types of red, blue, and yellow will provide warm or earthy colors. I recommend that you experiment to find out what you like best. It is perfectly fine to combine cool colors with warm colors. In the following directions, I will use the word "blue" for any shade of blue, including turquoise. Making different color wheels with different types of red, yellow, and blue is an interesting experiment that can show you how many color combinations can come from these three basic colors, depending on how the base dye colors are made.

Companies such as those listed in the Resources section, page 79, can usually give you a sheet of samples of each dye color they have and pamphlets that tell you what quantities they carry. These companies have minimum requirements for orders. They may be willing to send you sample fabric swatches. When you order, get some of the other colors you like so you can experiment with them as described in the various chapters. Catalogs have many good tips and more advanced information on dyes than is given here, and they are good resources if you have questions about specific items. You may want to read through this book before placing your order.

Color Wheels

A 12-step fabric color wheel can provide a handy reference (opposite page). Because all measuring instruments are slightly different, be sure that, when it says "scant," you use just under the amount given. After you have mixed your colors in the pickle jars, some jars may be more than half full. Pour out the dye until each jar is just under half full. You may still have some spillage when you put your fabric in the jar.

Color Wheel Recipes

Make red, blue, and yellow dye solutions as described in How to Make Dye Solution, page 17. From the three quart-sized containers, fill your pickle jars with these amounts:

Twelve-step fabric color wheel.

24-Step Color Wheel

Jar 1:   scant ½ c. red

Jar 2:   scant ½ c. red + 1 Tbsp. yellow

Jar 3:   ⅓ c. red + 2 Tbsp. yellow

Jar 4:   scant ⅓ c. red + scant ¼ c. yellow

Jar 5:   ¼ c. red + scant ⅓ c. yellow

Jar 6:   2 Tbsp. red + ⅓ c. yellow

Jar 7:   1 Tbsp. red + scant ½ c. yellow

Jar 8:   1 tsp. red + scant ½ c. yellow

Jar 9:   scant ½ c. yellow

Jar 10:   scant ½ c. yellow + 1 Tbsp. blue

Jar 11:   ⅓ c. yellow + 1 Tbsp. blue

Jar 12:   ¼ c. yellow + 1 Tbsp. blue

Jar 13:   2 Tbsp. yellow + ⅓ c. blue

Jar 14:   2 tsp. yellow + scant ½ c. blue

Jar 15:   scant ½ c. blue

Jar 16:   scant ½ c. blue + 1 tsp. red

Jar 17:   scant ½ c. blue + 1 Tbsp. red

Jar 18:   ⅓ c. blue + 2 Tbsp. red

Jar 19:   scant ⅓ c. blue + scant ¼ c. red

Jar 20:   scant ¼ c. blue + scant ⅓ c. red

Jar 21:   scant ¼ c. blue + ⅓ c. red

Jar 22:   3 Tbsp. blue + ⅓ c. red

Jar 23:   1 Tbsp. blue + scant ½ c. red

Jar 24:   1 tsp. blue + scant ½ c. red

12-Step Color Wheel

Jar 1:   scant ½ c. red

Jar 2:   3 Tbsp. red + ¼ c. yellow

Jar 3:   1 Tbsp. red + ⅓ c. yellow

Jar 4:   ½ tsp. red + scant ½ 39 yellow

Jar 5:   scant ½ c. yellow

Jar 6:   scant ½ c. yellow + 1 Tbsp. blue

Jar 7:   ⅛ c. yellow + ¼ c. blue

Jar 8:   scant ½ c. blue + 1 Tbsp. yellow

Jar 9:   scant ½ c. blue

Jar 10:   ⅓ c. blue + 3 Tbsp. red

Jar 11:   1 Tbsp. blue + ⅓ 39 red

Jar 12:   1 tsp. blue + scant ½ c. red

How to Pickle Fabrics

Assemble the equipment and supplies listed on pages 11 and 19.

Prepare fabric (1 hour)
• If you use fabric you have on hand, wash it first in hot water to which has been added ¼ cup Synthrapol soap to scour away any chemical residues or finishes. PFD fabric does not need this initial washing.

• Cut or tear the fabric into fat quarters and soak them in warm dye activator solution for at least 20 minutes to overnight. If you leave the fabric any longer, the chemicals in the dye activator can weaken your fabric.

Prepare dye solution (15 minutes)
• You can prepare the dye solutions while your fabric is soaking. Following the recipe given on page 17, prepare three quart-sized containers of dye solution in the  three primary colors (red or fuchsia, blue or turquoise, and yellow) inside your mixing box. Once the dye powder has been mixed into the chem water, you can remove the mixing box and your mask.

Figure 3. *Fill quart dyes with chem water and dye.*

Always wear a dust mask when working with powdered dyes.

Prepare jars of dye (20–30 minutes)
• Leave the jars in the box they came in until you are ready to pour the dye into them. Unscrew the  lids from the pickle jars and set the lids aside.

Figure 4. *Fill jars with dye solution.*

• Following the color-wheel recipe, pour dye solution into each jar (Figure 4). Mark your jars "Jar 1," "Jar 2," etc. The jars should be just under half full, so pour out any extra solution. It is okay if some of the jars are less than half full.

Fill jars with fabric (10 minutes)

Step 4

• Keep your gloves on. One by one, remove the fabrics from the dye activator solution and squeeze excess solution from the wet fat quarters (Figure 5). The fabrics should be very wet, but not dripping, so they will soak up the dye solution evenly. Try to create as many small wrinkles and crevices in the fabrics as you can while keeping them wet.

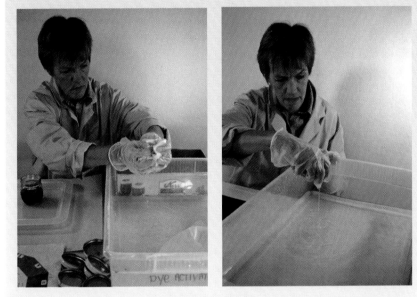

Figure 5. *Squeeze out a little of the excess dye activator solution.*

• With gloved hands and working in a bin or plastic tray with a lip, carefully insert the fabrics into the jars. Use a chopstick or spoon to push the fabrics down and around to completely soak them with dye solution (Figure 6).

• Screw the lids on tight and shake each jar. Replace the jars in the box.

Tip: If you prefer, you can put the wet fabrics in the jars before pouring the dye over them. Some colors will disperse more this way, giving the fabric a different look.

Figure 6. *Insert the wet fabrics into jars of dye solution.*

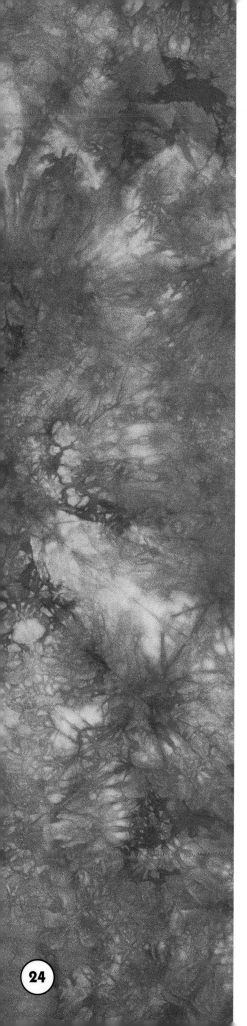

pickle-jar fabrics

Cure fabric (at least 2 hours up to 24 hours)

• It takes a little less than two hours for the dye to chemically bond with the fabric. The more fabric you squeeze into the jar, the more pronounced the patterns will be. That is why, for a fat quarter of fabric, a half-pint jar is just about right. It is important to put the fabric in very wet, push it around with a stick or spoon, and shake it well. This way, you are less likely to have white spots in your fabric.

• Let the fabric sit in the jars overnight to cure. If you can't get to it, you can leave it longer, but try not to leave it more than a few days because the chemicals can begin to weaken the fabric. In these small amounts, you can leave fabrics to cure longer than you can when using larger amounts because you are not exposing the fabric to as much of the dye activator solution.

Rinse and wash (30–60 minutes)

• Remove jar lids and put in a plastic bin for cleaning. Set the box of jars with dyed fabric pieces next to you by the washing machine.

• Fill your washing machine, set at a medium or large load, with hot water and add ¼ cup Synthrapol soap. Let the washer agitate to disperse the soap.

• Put on your gloves. Gently pull each fabric out of the jar and put it into the water. (You can pour any excess dye into the washer with the fabric.) As you're putting the fabric in the washer, occasionally close the washing machine lid and let the machine agitate a few moments to distribute the fabrics. Set the jars back in the box and put the lids in the plastic bin to be cleaned later. Complete this first wash-rinse cycle.

• Repeat the wash-rinse cycle three times, adding Synthrapol to the first two cycles. I have found that you can mix all the colors in the machine without hand rinsing first, and the Synthrapol will keep them from bleeding onto one another. Check your rinse water the second time you wash. If it has any color, wash a third time with Synthrapol before proceeding to the final wash.

I cannot emphasize enough the importance of running your fabrics through at least three entire wash-rinse cycles to make them colorfast. The fabric, especially if mercerized, will not fade.

Step 7

Dry (20–30 minutes)
• Dry the fabrics thoroughly in a hot dryer. The heat further sets the dye, as does the heat from the next step.

Step 8

Steam press (30 minutes)
• Ironing will bring out the mottled appearance of the colors. You will be amazed that a fabric which looks ugly when it comes out of the dryer can look so luminous and beautiful after being pressed.

Bin Dyeing

Tip: After using any of the bin-dyeing methods, put the top on the bin to keep the fabric moist. Cure it for at least two hours to overnight. To finish bin-dyed fabrics, follow the instructions in Chapter Two, step six (page 24).

Color mixing

• You can soak any amount of PFD fabric in dye activator solution, then place the wet fabric in a shallow plastic bin.

• Using your gloved fingers, make as many little wrinkles and indentations as possible, squeezing the fabric toward one end of the bin. In this way, you can dye a single large piece of fabric or several smaller ones.

• Then pour your dye solution, in any color or mixed colors, into the bin. Using gloved fingers, push the fabric down in the dye, really mashing the fabric into the dye solution.

• Prop the bin up on one side. The tilted bin will allow the dye solution to penetrate the fabrics in a gradated fashion.

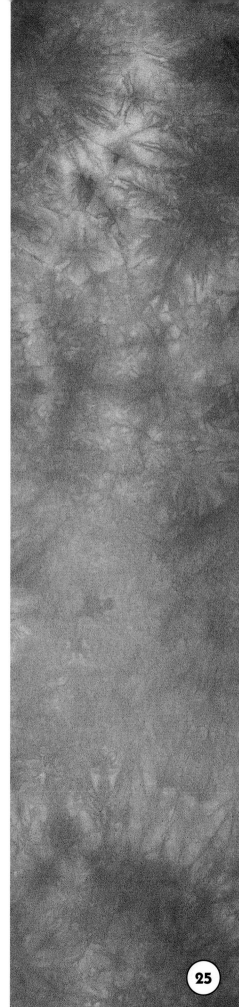

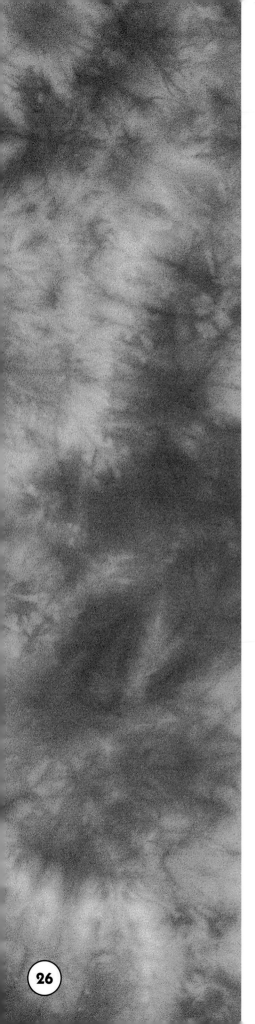

pickle-jar fabrics

One-color gradation

• Pour a strong, dark color at one end of the tub and gradually mash the fabric into the dye so that the color is lighter toward the last end of the length of fabric. Prop the bin at an angle to retain the gradation.

Color-to-color gradation

• Using a propped bin, you can also make a color-to-color gradation. For example, place your prepared fabric in the bin and pour blue at one end and yellow at the other. Work the dyes toward the middle with your gloved fingers to produce a blue-green-yellow gradation, with all the subtle colors in between. With this method you can use any amount of dye solution you want, in light, medium, or dark batch recipes.

The amount of fabric you need depends on the size of the finished piece. I like to work with fat quarters cut to 18" x 18" or, if I need bigger pieces, I cut them 44" x 44". It is not necessary to work only with squares. You can achieve interesting results with odd sizes, too. The size of the zipper-locked bags needed with also vary, as will the amount of dye solution. For 18" x 18" pieces, use the 12-step recipe on page 21. For 44" x 44" pieces, double the 12-step recipe amounts.

Twist and squirt

• Twist your soaked fabric into any shape you want. Use a funnel to put dye solution into squirt bottles, then squirt dye into the fabric in various places. Place the fabric in a zipper-locked plastic bag and squeeze it with your hands to make sure the dye solution reaches all the crevices.

Tip: To get earthy colors from your basic red, yellow, and blue, mix a little of the opposite color on the color wheel. Opposites will produce various shades of brown, rust, green, gray, tan, etc. Adding ½ tsp. black dye powder to your dye solution also tones the colors, creating more of an earthy look. If, however, you want to get a certain color you see in the dye company's charts, use the pre-mixed dye powder to be more accurate in achieving a specific color.

Pickle-dyed reds

Double New York Beauty block by Jaye Lapachete, Daly City, California.

pickle-jar fabrics

Pickle-dyed purples and magenta, fold-dyed green center
Pineapple block by Becky Wall, Wilmington, Delaware.

pickle-jar fabrics

Pickle-dyed purple, fold-dyed green
Untitled by Marguerite Borck, Pincorring, Michigan.

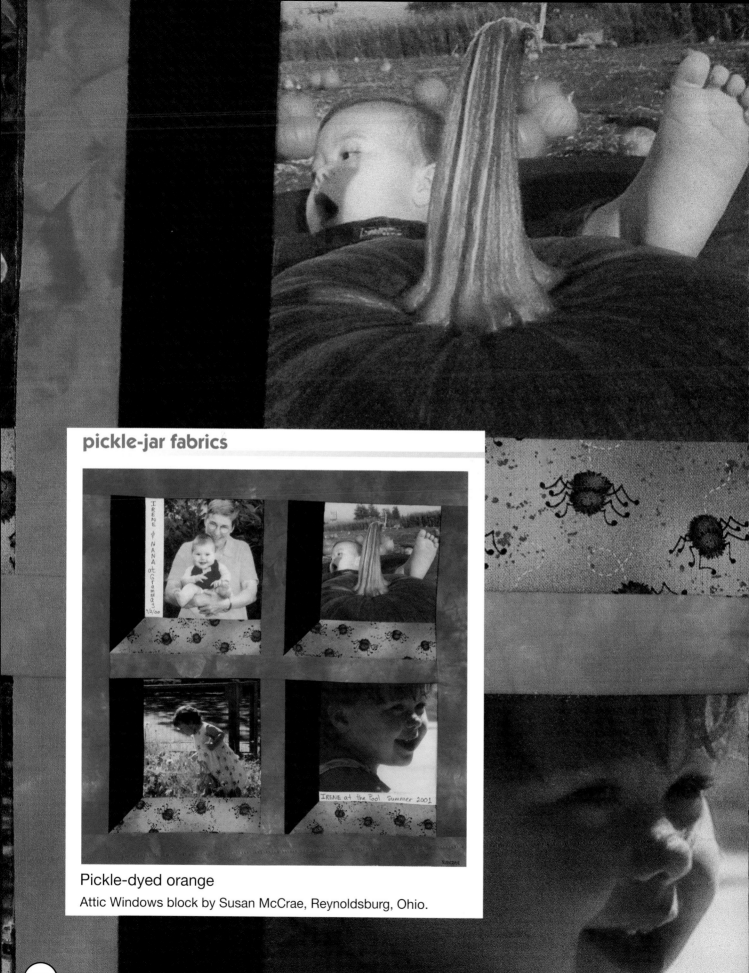

pickle-jar fabrics

Pickle-dyed orange
Attic Windows block by Susan McCrae, Reynoldsburg, Ohio.

Pickle-dyed orange wings

BUTTERFLY* by Susan McRae, Reynoldsburg, Ohio.

*Butterfly pattern from Playful
Patchwork Projects by K.P. Kids.

fold-dyed fabrics

Fold-dyed anvil shape, pickle-dyed dark green

Anvil block by Barbara Bachmann, Rouge River, Oregon.

chapter 3

Fold-Dyed Fabrics

For this method, you will not need jars. You may want to get small amounts of ready-made dye from a catalog or manufacturer if you want your fold-dyed fabrics to contain certain colors that may be difficult or time-consuming to mix yourself. The steps for this process vary a little from the pickle jar fabrics method, so it's a good idea to read through them before proceeding.

I cannot give you a recipe that will produce exactly the fabric you see illustrated. Each piece will be a surprise, though most will give you relatively the same patterns as shown in the samples. I have included eight different folding methods and their results and have also provided some photographs of other fabrics I have made by using my own spontaneous folding methods.

Additional Supplies (see also page 11)

- Fabric: PFD fabric cut into 18" or 44" squares
- Funnel
- Several small squirt bottles
- Quart-sized zipper-locked plastic bags. (You will need as many bags as pieces of fabrics to be dyed.)
- Small plastic-coated clips or clothespins
- Extra half-quart or quart containers

fold-dyed fabrics

How to Fold-Dye

Assemble the equipment and supplies listed on page 11 and 33.

Step 1

Prepare fabric (1 hour)
• If you use fabric you have on hand, wash it first in hot water to which has been added ¼ c. Synthrapol soap to scour away any chemical residues or finishes. PFD fabric from the dye companies does not need this initial washing.

• Cut your fabric into 18" or 44" squares. You can also use leftover pieces from other projects, and if you like, you can overdye pickle-jar fabrics with the fold-dyed process. For spontaneous folding, you can use any size piece you want. If you use three quarts or several smaller containers of dye solution, you should be able to dye about six or more yards of fabric. If you don't have that much fabric to dye, the dye solution will keep in a cool place for several weeks as long as it is not mixed with the dye activator solution.

• Take your washed and dried fabric pieces to the ironing board. You can start with a square, rectangle, or triangle. Most of the examples start with an 18" square. Fold the fabric according to the directions or, for a more spontaneous-looking piece, make folds however you like. Each time you fold, steam press the piece well. You can experiment with all types of folds. Even folding two pieces the same way will not yield identical results.

• Fold your fabric until it will fit in a quart-sized plastic zipper-locked bag (or a larger bag if you are using larger pieces). Clip the fabric piece with plastic-coated clothespins to keep it folded while it is soaking in the dye activator solution (Figure 7). Remove the clips to begin the dyeing process.

• Place dye activator solution in a long, shallow plastic tub. Make sure the solution is warm. (See page 16 for tips on warming used solution that may have become cold.) Carefully place your folded

Figure 7. *Folded fabrics, pressed and ready to soak. Use plastic clips to hold the folds.*

fabrics in the tub of solution. Let them soak for at least 20 minutes. They can soak overnight if necessary.

Prepare dye solution (30 minutes)

Step 2

Follow the directions on page 22 to prepare your containers of dye solution in the colors of your choice. If you want more colors, mix your chem water (recipe on page 16) and pour it into containers with spouts. Fill the containers with chem water and add dye powder, according to the amount suggested on page 17, to each container. Remember to put on your mask and gloves and work in your mixing box when mixing the dye powder into the chem water.

Prepare fabric (up to 1 hour)

Step 3

• Keep your gloves on and your plastic bags nearby. Using a funnel, transfer the dye solutions into squirt bottles (Figure 8). You can mix different colors together if you'd like to experiment.

Figure 8. *Use a funnel to pour dye solution into squirt bottles.*

• Working in a plastic tub (placed in a utility sink if possible), carefully move one piece of fabric into the tub. Keep it dripping wet. Remove the clips and set them aside. Squirt dye solution along the folds (Figure 9). If you see dots or hard edges, smooth them with your fingers. Carefully, open the fabric a little bit and squirt some dye along the folds and edges. Use your fingers to spread the dye as before. Close the folded fabric back up again. Using another color, if you like, gently open the fabric so you can squirt dye solution into the center of the

Figure 9. *Squirt dye along the folds.*

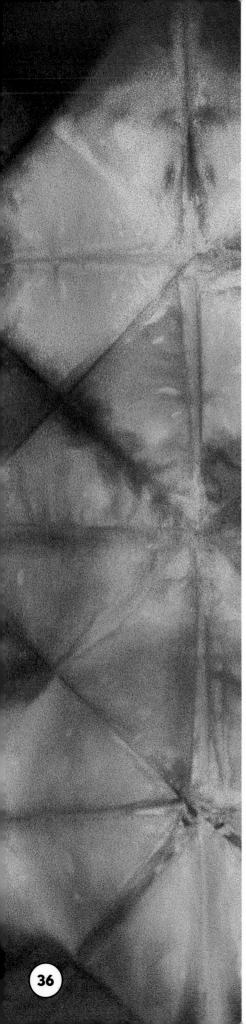

fold-dyed fabrics

fabric in different layers (Figure 10). Use your gloved hands to press down, making sure that the dye solution penetrates through all the folds (Figure 11).

Figure 10. *Squirt dye in the center between the folds.*

It takes a lot of pressing to make sure you don't get white spots where you don't want them. You may want more pastel areas with darker lines along the folds, or you may want deep, dark color throughout, with the fold lines showing more faintly. One of the reasons your fabric should be soaking wet is to help the dye solution penetrate all the layers. The urea helps accomplish this also. If you use smaller pieces of fabric to begin with, there will not be as many layers to pene-

Figure 11. *Press with gloved fingers to distribute the dye solution.*

Figure 12. *Place the folded fabric into a plastic zipper-locked bag.*

trate, and it will be easier to get deep, dark color throughout, if that is what you want.

• Carefully slide the folded fabric into a plastic bag (Figure 12). You may want to squirt more dye solution into the bag, just to add more depth and penetration if you have a large piece (Figure 13). Close the bag and set it, bottom side down,

Figure 13. *Squirt more dye into the plastic bag.*

into a plastic bin to cure. You may want to squeeze and squish the bag around some more to further encourage the dye solution to penetrate all the layers.

Tip: It may look as if all you're going to have is a blob of muddy color, but trust the process and be generous with your dye solution. You'll be amazed at how the colors settle into the folds and separate.

 **Cure the fabric (at least 2 hours up to overnight or more if necessary)**
Step 4
• Set your tub of plastic bags aside in a warm place to cure.

 **Wash and dry (2 hours)**
Step 5
• Fill your washing machine, set on medium or large load, with hot water and add ¼ c. of Synthrapol; agitate.

• Put on gloves. Empty the plastic bags into the water, stopping every few minutes to agitate. You can let the dye solution go into the washer, and you can mix whatever colors you have. The Synthrapol, when thoroughly agitated into the water, will keep the fabrics from bleeding onto one another.

• Run your washing machine through three wash-rinse cycles, adding Synthrapol to the first two wash cycles.

• Dry the fabrics in a hot dryer.

• Steam press each piece of fabric. You will see that the pattern of the folds and the colors you have dyed will become brighter and clearer, and steam pressing will further set the color into the fabric. If you have a fabric that you don't particularly like, you can start over and either use the pickle-jar method described on page 19–26 or re-fold the piece and use different colors for fold dyeing. You do not need to wash the fabric first when you over-dye.

fold-dyed fabrics

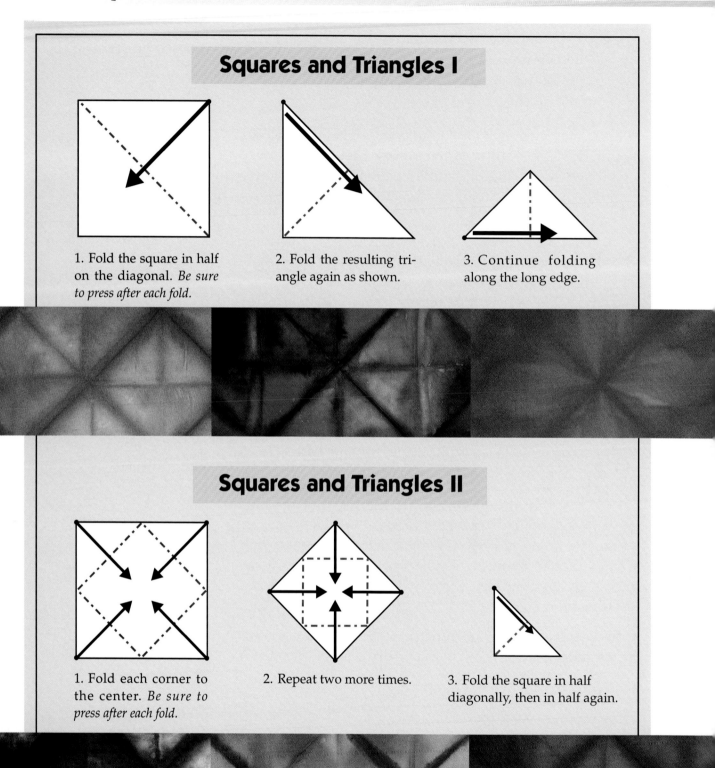

Squares and Triangles I

1. Fold the square in half on the diagonal. *Be sure to press after each fold.*

2. Fold the resulting triangle again as shown.

3. Continue folding along the long edge.

Squares and Triangles II

1. Fold each corner to the center. *Be sure to press after each fold.*

2. Repeat two more times.

3. Fold the square in half diagonally, then in half again.

Squares and Triangles III

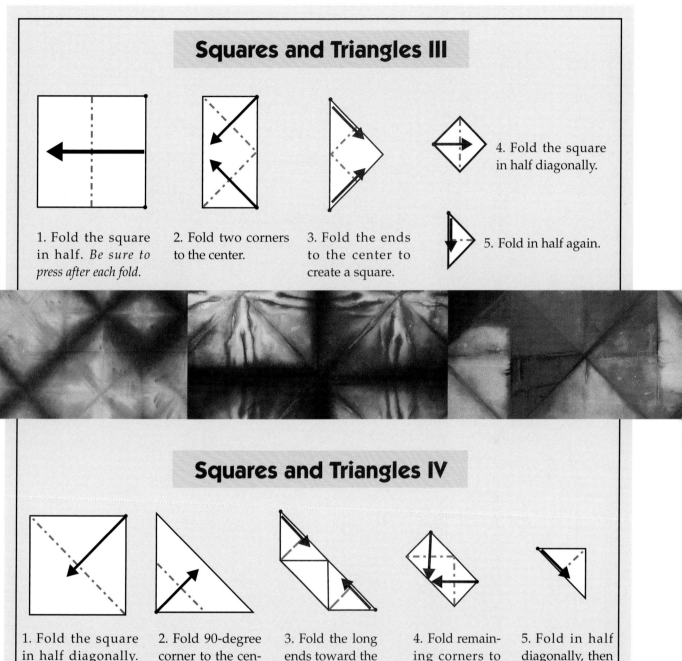

1. Fold the square in half. *Be sure to press after each fold.*

2. Fold two corners to the center.

3. Fold the ends to the center to create a square.

4. Fold the square in half diagonally.

5. Fold in half again.

Squares and Triangles IV

1. Fold the square in half diagonally. *Be sure to press after each fold.*

2. Fold 90-degree corner to the center of the opposite side.

3. Fold the long ends toward the center.

4. Fold remaining corners to the center.

5. Fold in half diagonally, then in half again if possible.

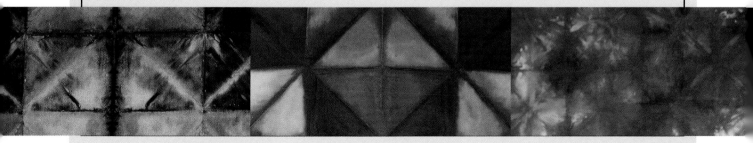

fold-dyed fabrics

Squares and Triangles V

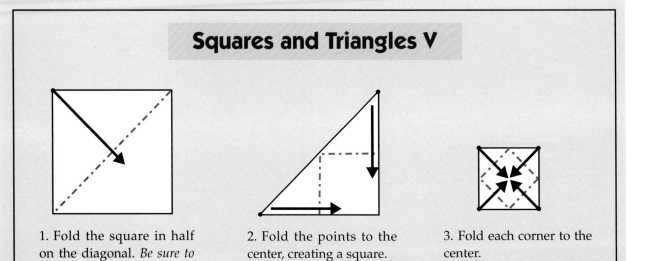

1. Fold the square in half on the diagonal. *Be sure to press after each fold.*

2. Fold the points to the center, creating a square.

3. Fold each corner to the center.

Squares

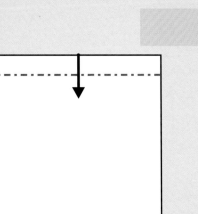

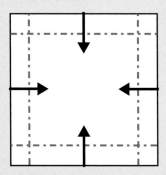

1. Fold one side over 2". *Be sure to press after each fold.*

2. Moving clockwise, repeat on each side until you have a smaller square.

3. Fold the square in half.

Accordion Fan

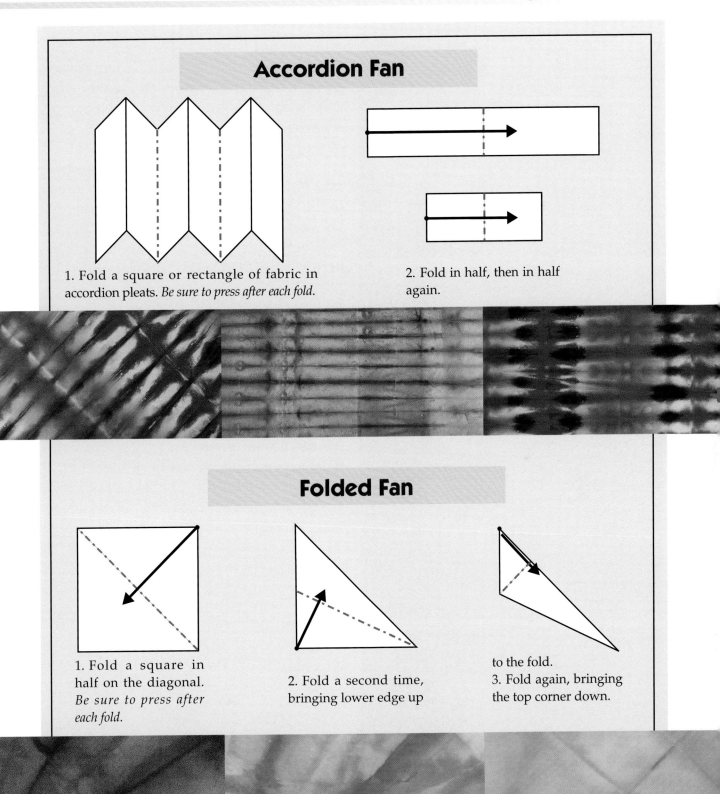

1. Fold a square or rectangle of fabric in accordion pleats. *Be sure to press after each fold.*

2. Fold in half, then in half again.

Folded Fan

1. Fold a square in half on the diagonal. *Be sure to press after each fold.*

2. Fold a second time, bringing lower edge up to the fold.

3. Fold again, bringing the top corner down.

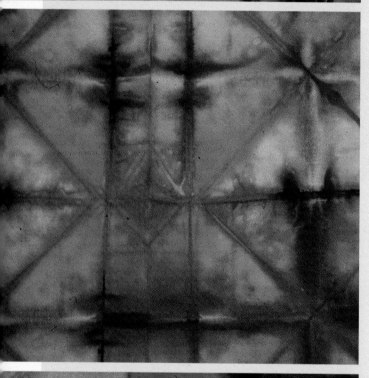

fold-dyed fabrics

Now, you do some experimenting. Try different folds, use different sizes of fabric pieces. This is the fun part, for you can play with whatever folds you choose and see what wonderful patterns develop.

If you want to duplicate your patterns, take notes as you fold, and draw pictures of the size and shape of your fabric pieces and how you fold them. Be sure to number the folds in your drawing and place arrows indicating the direction of the folds.

Remember, as you fold the fabric, iron the folds, then soak the piece thoroughly in dye activator solution. Use a squeeze bottle to dye your folded piece. When you place your fabric in the zipper-locked bag to cure, squirt extra dye in and squeeze the piece with your hands to be sure all the dye penetrates the fabric. Then continue as you would for any fold-dyed fabrics. Good luck! I would love to see what you come up with!

fold-dyed fabrics

Fold-dyed light blue, pickle-dyed dark blue
Nine Patch block by Wendy J. Crawford, Beavercreek, Oregon.

fold-dyed fabrics

Fold-dyed greens

Pinwheel block by C. Merchant, Corinth, Maine.

fold-dyed fabrics

Fold-dyed leaves
Autumn Leaves block by Barbara Bachmann, Rogue River, Oregon.

tie-dyed fabrics

Fan-folded borders with tie-dyed center and corners

BERRY PASSION SPIRAL, by Julie Z. Stiller, Boulder Creek, California.

chapter 4
Tie-Dyed Fabrics

Tie dyeing is easy to do, can create amazing effects, and can be used on PFD tee shirts, scarves, and other clothing. This is a great method for creating gifts for the kids in your life. Before beginning, follow the directions on page 17 for making dye solutions in your chosen colors. Assemble the basic supplies listed on page 11 and below.

Additional Supplies (see also page 11)

- Fabric: PFD fabric in squares (Use any size up to one yard. If you use the amounts of dye shown on page 21, this recipe will dye up to six yards of fabric.)
- One-gallon container with pour spout
- Three quart containers with pour spouts
- Several squeeze bottles with tops
- Funnel for filling squeeze bottles
- Twine (Waxed is best. Many people use dental floss.)
- Scissors for removing twine
- Plastic tray with a lip. (This type of container is ideal because it prevents the dye solution from running off the sides. If you don't have one, work in a plastic bin.)
- Several gallon-sized plastic zipper-locked bags (These can an be smaller for smaller amounts of fabric.)
- Retayne®
- Dowel for twisting fabric (½" diameter for fat quarters)

tie-dyed fabrics

How to Tie-Dye

Assemble the equipment and supplies listed on pages 11 and 47.

Prepare fabric (30 minutes)
• Cut or tear your pieces of fabric. For tie-dyed patterns, squares are easiest to work with. Soak fabric in dye activator solution for at least 20 minutes to overnight or longer.

Step 1

Manipulate and tie your fabric (1–2 hours)
• The following directions show how to manipulate the wet fabric to achieve different types of effects for tie-dyed fabrics. As you finish each piece, slip it into a zipper-locked plastic bag, lock it, and place it in a plastic tub for curing. For some of the patterns, be careful during this process so that the colors do not mix together too much.

Step 2

Cure, wash, and dry fabric (2 hours to overnight)
• After allowing the fabric to cure at least two hours to overnight or more, fill your washing machine (medium to heavy load) with hot water and ¼ c. Synthrapol. Agitate.

Step 3

• Cut the twine off and throw it away. Place the fabric in the water. Run the washing machine through three wash-rinse cycles, adding some Retayne, according to the bottle directions, to the last wash.

• Dry the fabrics in a hot dryer and steam press.

Tie-Dyed Patterns

All of the patterns can be made by using any dye solution colors you like. I encourage you to experiment with many different colors to create a complete palette with which to work.

Tip: Small squares of fabric are a little more difficult to work with than large squares because of the twisting, turning, and tying involved. But you should be able to get good results from squares as small as 12", 14", or 18".

Yin yang

• Place your index fingers on the fabric, as shown. Pulling in opposite directions, turn the fabric clockwise. Reposition your fingers as shown in Figure 14, then turn the fabric clockwise again. Continue in this manner until all the fabric has been taken up.

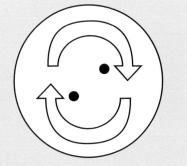

Figure 14. *Place your index fingers on the fabric.*

Figure 15. *Place fingers at dots and pull outward as you twist fabric clockwise.*

• Squeeze the shape together and form it into a log shape (Figure 16). Use twine to tie the shape tightly in several places (Figure 17).

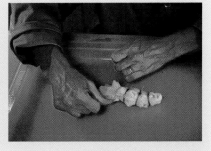

Figure 16. *Squeeze the twisted fabric into a log shape.*

Figure 17. *Use twine to tie the shape tightly in several places.*

• Working in a bin, apply dye with squeeze bottles (Figure 18). Press the dye with your gloved fingers to eliminate hard lines. Bag your fabric then refer to Step 3 for finishing

Figure 18. *Squirt dye into each section.*

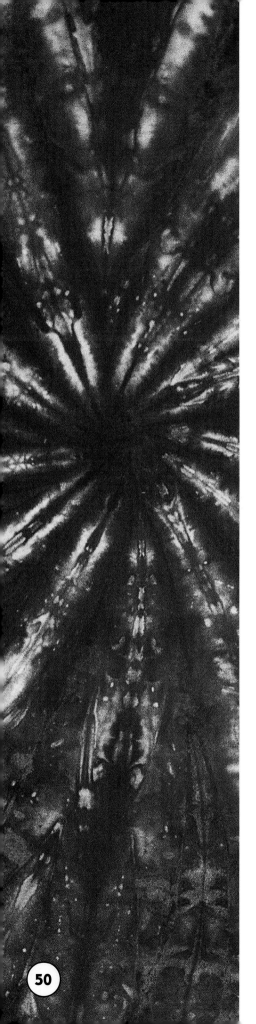

tie-dyed fabrics

Central sunburst

Figure 19. *Pick up the fabric from the center.*

• Pick the fabric piece up from the center and smooth it into long folds (Figure 19).

• Use twine to tie the piece in sections (Figure 20).

• Squirt dye into the sections and use your gloved fingers to eliminate hard edges (Figure 21).

Figure 20. *Tie the folded piece in sections.*

Figure 21. *Dye the sections with squeeze bottle.*

Mirror-image fan

• Fold the fabric piece in half diagonally (Figure 22).

• Place the end of a dowel in one corner (Figure 23). Turn the fabric clockwise around the dowel until all the fabric is taken up.

• Remove the dowel and shape the coiled fabric into a circle, arranging the folds as you go (Figure 24).

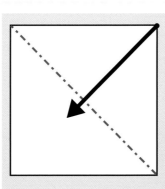

Figure 22. *Fold the fabric square in half diagonally.*

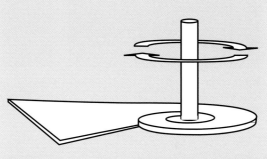

Figure 23. *Place tip of dowel in one corner and twist fabric clockwise around dowel.*

• Tie the resulting shape in a bundle as shown in Figure 25.

• Squirt dye into each section (Figure 26). Bag the fabric then refer to Step 3.

Figure 24. *Press the shape into a circle.*

Figure 25. *Tie shape in sections.*

Figure 26. *Squirt dye into the sections, then place the fabric in a zipper-locked plastic bag to cure.*

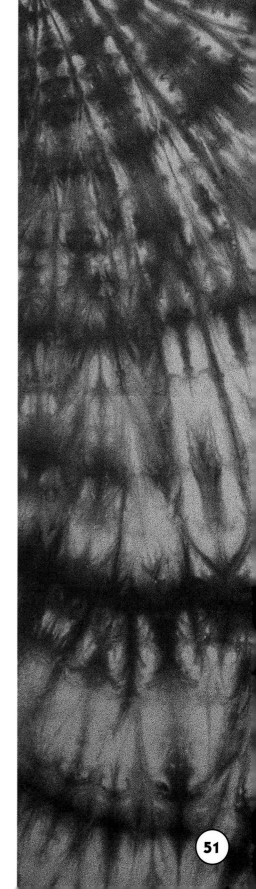

tie-dyed fabrics

Spiral sunburst

• Place a dowel use or your fingers in the center of a piece of fabric and slowly twist the fabric clockwise until all the fabric is taken up (Figure 27).

• Arrange the resulting shape into a circle (Figure 28).

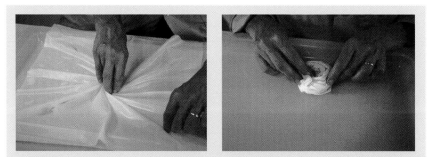

Figure 27. *Twist to make the shape, arranging folds as you go.*   **Figure 28.** *Arrange twisted fabric in a circle.*

• Tie the circle in sections (Figure 29).
• Squirt dye into each of the sections (Figure 30), then place fabric in a zipper-locked plastic bag to cure. Refer to Step 3, page 48, for finishing

Figure 29. *Tie off.*   **Figure 30.** *Squirt dye in sections.*

Some dye books caution you about mixing complementary colors, that is, those that are opposite on the color wheel, red and green, yellow and purple, blue and orange. This caution is often given especially for tie-dyeing and would apply if you want clear colors, for instance, by keeping red and green from mixing. However, I like the look of a little earthy color mixed in among the brights. So you will have to experiment yourself and see what appeals to you. When you do mix complementary colors, it is better if one of those colors is dominant, because a one-to-one mix of complementary colors yields a rather muddy gray.

Shibori-style Tie-Dye

The following simple method will produce Shibori-like patterns. Shibori is a Japanese style of tie-dyeing. You can use the recipes on page 21 for your dye solutions and select dyes in any colors you choose.

Assemble the items listed below and on page 11. You will not need jars, however. You may want to get small amounts of ready-made dye from a catalog or manufacturer if you want your fold-dyed fabrics to contain certain colors that may be difficult or time-consuming to mix yourself. The steps for this process vary a little from the pickle-jar method, so it's best to read through these steps before proceeding.

> **Tip:** You may want to experiment with the size of your PVC pipe. Try a 1" or 2" diameter and see what happens to the pattern.

Additional Supplies

- Fabric: Strips cut or torn on the lengthwise grain, 10" wide and up to a half yard long
- Several ½" diameter, 10" lengths of PVC pipe
- Plastic tub

How to Dye Shibori-style

Assemble the equipment and supplies listed above and on page 11.

Prepare fabric (15–20 minutes)
Soak the cut or torn fabric strips in the dye activator solution for at least 20 minutes to overnight.

Mix your dye solutions (20 minutes)
Mix a gallon of chem water, then pour it into several containers, or just one, depending on what color or colors you want. Using your gloves, mask, apron, and mixing box, add the

dye powder to the containers of chem water and mix well. You can now put away your mixing box and remove your mask, but keep your gloves on. Using a funnel, pour your colors into the squeeze bottles.

Roll your fabric and dye it (30 minutes)

1. Take one piece of fabric out of the dye activator solution and, holding it over a plastic tub or sink, roll the strip onto a PVC pipe (Figure 31). Don't worry about wrinkles. They will create interesting patterns. As you roll, use a squirt bottle to squirt a fine line of color along the pipe once, if you like (Figure 32). Use your gloved fingers to squeeze and spread the dye.

Figure 31. *Roll the fabric onto a PVC pipe.*

2. When you have rolled the length of cloth onto the pipe, secure it by tying twine on one end, winding it tightly around the pipe diagonally to the other end, and tying it off (Figure 33). Squirt dye solution over the tied fabric (Figure 34). Place the fabric-wound PVC pipe in the plastic tub.

Figure 32. *Squirt dye along the fabric roll.*

Figure 33. *Wrap the pipe with twine.*

Figure 34. *Squirt more dye along the pipe.*

3. Squeeze the fabric toward the center of the pipe as tightly as possible (Figure 35).

4. Squirt more dye solution into a gallon-sized plastic bag, then put the fabric pipe in the bag and lock it shut (Figure 36). Place the bag in a plastic bin for curing.

Figure 35. *Squeeze the fabric toward the center.*   **Figure 36.** *Put the pipe in a plastic bag for curing.*

Cure, wash, and dry fabric (2 hours to overnight)

Step 4

1. After allowing the fabric to cure at least two hours up to overnight or more, fill your washing machine (medium to heavy load) with hot water and ¼ c. Synthrapol. Agitate. With gloved hands, cut the twine off the pipes and throw it away. Holding the pipe over the washing machine, unroll the fabric into the water. Set the pipe aside. Run the washing machine through three wash-rinse cycles, adding Synthrapol to the first two wash cycles.

2. Dry the fabrics in a hot dryer and steam press.

tie-dyed fabrics

Tie-dyed star

Framed Star block by Becky Wall, Wilmington, Delaware.

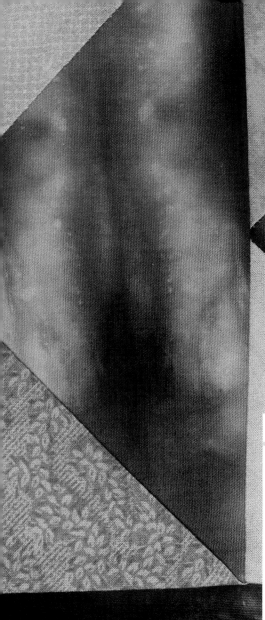

Tie-dyed magenta and turquoise
Dutchman's Puzzle block by Marilyn Herzog, Houston, Texas.

tie-dyed fabrics

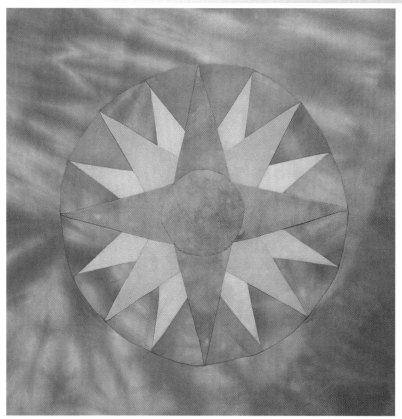

Tie-dyed blue background with pickled fabrics in star

Star block by Becky Wall, Wilmington, Delaware.

Tie-dyed center and corners, fold-dyed turquoise
FLASHBACK, by Sharon Clarke, Sierra Vista, Arizona.

stencils and sprays

Stenciled leaves over pickle-dyed fabrics
by Cherie Ekholm, Redmond, Washington.

chapter 5

Stencils and Sprays

You can take your previously dyed fabrics one step further by adding stenciled designs. This book provides just a short introduction to all the many ways you can manipulate your fabrics to achieve amazing and unique patterns. Just using the methods described can yield yards of fabric to keep you busy making unique quilts for a long time. Try some of these techniques, then consider attending a workshop or getting books to help you reach the next stage of mastery in manipulating fabrics.

Additional Supplies (see also page 11)

- Fabric: PFD fabric cut into any sized square.
  (You can use your previously pickled fabrics if you like.)
- Several squeeze bottles with tops
- Plastic bin, tray, or sink in which to work
- Plastic sheets (can use garbage bags) to put over your stenciled fabric to keep moist while curing
- Stencils (These can be store bought, or you can cut them yourself from template plastic or clear plastic shelf liner.)
- Natural sea sponge, fat stencil brush, or sponge roller
- Small plastic spray bottles
- Good ventilation (This is a good project to do outdoors.)
- Mask for spraying
- Afterfix® (Get the smallest bottle you can find.)
- Masking tape
- Plastic bowls for mixing colors
- Print paste solution (see page 14)
- Paint brush about 1" wide to use with Afterfix

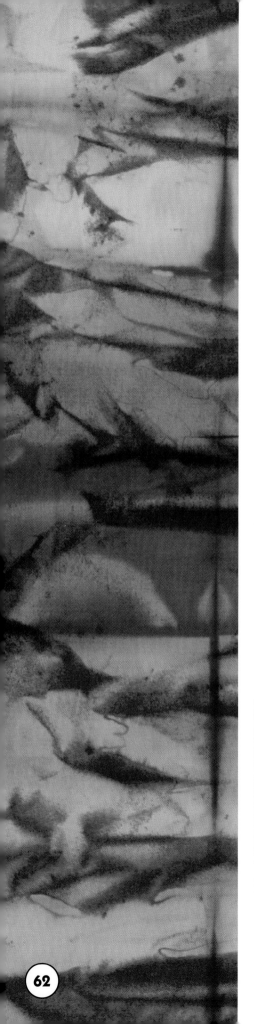

stencils and sprays

Sponge or Brush Painting

Step 1

Prepare print paste solution (day before)
• Following the instructions that come with the chemical, make your print paste solution.

Step 2

Prepare fabric (30 minutes)
• Cut your fabric into squares or rectangles. You may want to use fabric from your pickled or fold-dyed methods.

• Prepare some dye activator solution (see page 16) and place your cut fabric pieces in the warm solution to soak for at least 20 minutes to overnight.

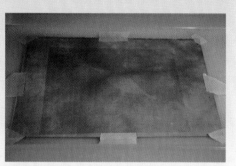

Figure 37. *Tape a fabric piece to a flat surface.*

• Take the fabric pieces out of the solution and let them dry. Press them flat.

• Place one of the fabric pieces on a tray or bin and tape the fabric in place with masking tape (Figure 37). Place the tray or bin on a table that has been covered with plastic.

Step 3

Make your stencils (30 minutes)
• From template plastic (or shelf liner), cut a square or rectangle larger than the object you want to trace. Trace a drawing of an object, such as a leaf or geometric shape, on the template material. If you use clear plastic shelf liner, draw on the paper side (Figure 38).

Figure 38. *Draw or trace a shape on template material.*

• Cut out the shape and put it aside (Figure 39). The square or rectangle left after cutting out the shape is your stencil.

Tip: You can cut several stencils from a large square or rectangle of plastic or opaque shelf liner to create all your stencils at once.

Figure 39. *Using a sharp box-cutter-type knife, cut out the shape.*

Step 4

Apply stencils and dye (one hour)

• Pour dye solution, in the colors you want to use, into plastic bowls. Add print paste solution to thicken the dye (Figure 40).

Figure 40. *Mix print paste solution into the dye solution to thicken it, as needed.*

• Place the stencil where you want the object on the fabric. If you are using template plastic, tape it over the fabric (Figure 41). If you are using shelf liner, peel off the paper backing to adhere the stencil to the fabric (Figure 42).

Figure 41. *Hold the stencil firmly and tape it over the fabric.*

• Dip a small piece of sponge, a small sponge paint roller, a sponge stencil pouncer, or a stiff stencil brush into the thickened dye solution. Tap it on a paper towel to remove excess dye.

Figure 42. *Peel the backing from the shelf liner and press the stencil firmly over the fabric.*

stencils and sprays

• Carefully pounce color on the open area of your stencil with your sponge or brush, experimenting with different pressures. Be careful that the dye solution is thick enough that it doesn't bleed under the stencil. Periodically clean off the stencil plastic with paper towels (Figure 43).

Figure 43. *Wipe away excess dye with a paper towel.*

• Cover the stenciled area with plastic and set the piece aside to cure until dry. You can then apply another coat with the same or a different color, if you like.

• When the stenciled area is covered to the degree you want and it is completely dry, paint over it with Afterfix and let it dry thoroughly (Figure 44).

• Repeat the dye process as desired, moving around the fabric to make stenciled objects in different places. You

Figure 44. *After the shape has dried, paint it with Afterfix.*

can experiment by lightly sponging only part of the object on the fabric so it looks transparent and appears to float.

Tip: If your stencil design has several different cut-outs, such as flower petals and leaves, you can dye them at the same time by using different dye colors in the cut-outs.

• Remove your stencil and allow the fabric to air dry at least two hours to overnight or longer. Fill your washing machine (set for a medium to heavy load) with hot water and ¼ cup Synthrapol. Agitate. Run the washing machine through three wash-rinse cycles, adding Synthrapol to the first two wash cycles.

• Fill your washing machine (set for a medium to heavy load) with hot water and ¼ cup Synthrapol.

• Dry the fabrics in a hot dryer and steam press them.

Spray Painting

- Cut your PFD fabrics into squares.

- Soak the squares in dye activator solution (page 16) at least 20 minutes to overnight or longer.

- Arrange a square of wet fabric on a tray or flat waterproof surface, such as a plastic bin (Figure 45). Arrange the fabric any way you want – scrunched, swirled, pinched, etc. You can do this randomly or in any repeated pattern you like.

Figure 45. *Arrange your fabric randomly on the tray.*

- Using plastic bowls, mix some dye solution with print paste mix so you have a slightly thickened solution.

- Use a funnel to fill a spray bottle with the slightly thickened dye solution.

Tip: Place your dust mask on and be sure all surfaces are covered with plastic. (This is a good step to do outdoors). Use gloves and any other protective gear you have to prevent over-spray from getting on other surfaces. Be sure, if you are indoors, that there is very good ventilation so that dye sprayed over the fabric does not stay in the air.

- Very lightly spray the fabric with dye solution (Figure 46). You can go over the fabric again to make it darker or add other colors.

- Cover the fabric with plastic, or if you are using a bin, put the cover on. Cure the fabric by keeping it moist for at least two hours to overnight.

- Fill your washing machine (medium to heavy load) with hot water and ¼ cup Synthrapol. Agitate. Add your fabrics and run the washing machine through three wash-rinse cycles, adding Synthrapol to the first two wash cycles.

- Dry in a hot dryer and steam press.

Figure 46. *Making sure the area is protected, spray your fabric lightly.*

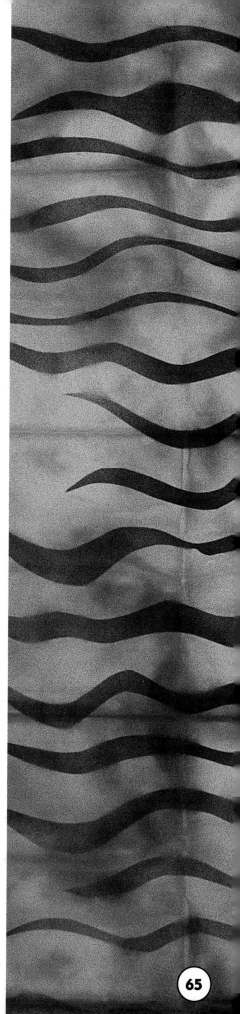

stencils and sprays

Spray on Flat Fabric

This method combines the flat look of stenciled fabric with the speckled look of spraying with thickened dye.

• Spray thickened dye solution on a stencil that has been firmly adhered to prepared fabric (Figure 47).

• Remove the stencil and the shape appears (Figure 48).

• Proceed with the curing, drying, and washing steps as with any dyed piece.

Figure 47. *Spray thickened dye solution over the stencil.*

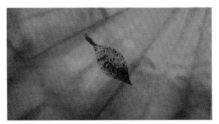

Figure 48. *Remove the stencil to reveal the shape.*

stencils and sprays

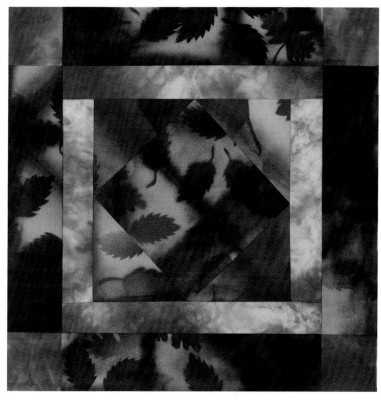

Stenciled leaves over fold-dyed fabric, pickled inner border and corner squares

Amish miniature block by Leslie Blair, Boulder, Colorado.

stencils and sprays

Stenciling over fold-dyed fabric

Double Square block by Barbara Bachmann, Rogue River, Oregon.

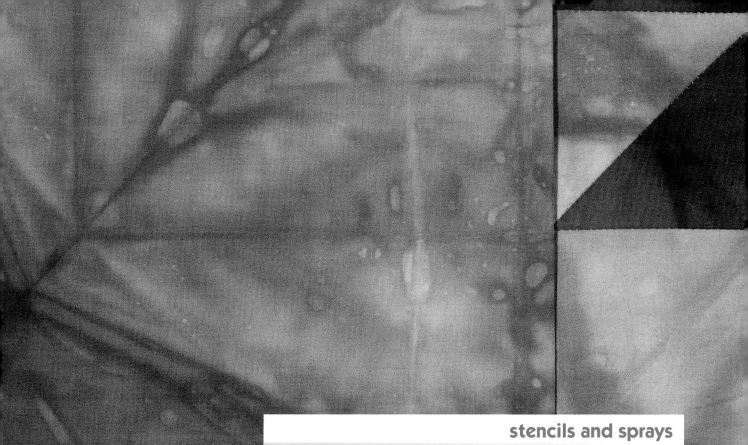

Stenciled leaves over fold-dyed fabrics
Maple Leaves block by Cherie Ekholm, Redmond, Washington.

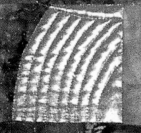

stencils and sprays

JOIE DE VIVRE II

Seasonal Quilt Series, with stenciled fabrics, by the author.

gallery

gallery

WOLF PUP, 32" x 36", Wildlife Series, by the author. Fabrics: pickle-dyed pieces in stained-glass border and strip-pieced foliage.

JOIE DE VIVRE I, 50" x 64", Seasonal Quilt Series, by the author. This series expresses joy in the changing light and colors in Colorado. Fabrics: pickle-dyed and stenciled pieces, with silk, lamé, and photographic imagery.

JOIE DE VIVRE III, 40" x 47", Seasonal Quilt Series, by the author. Fabrics: pickle-dyed, fold-dyed, and stenciled pieces, with commercial cottons and lamé.

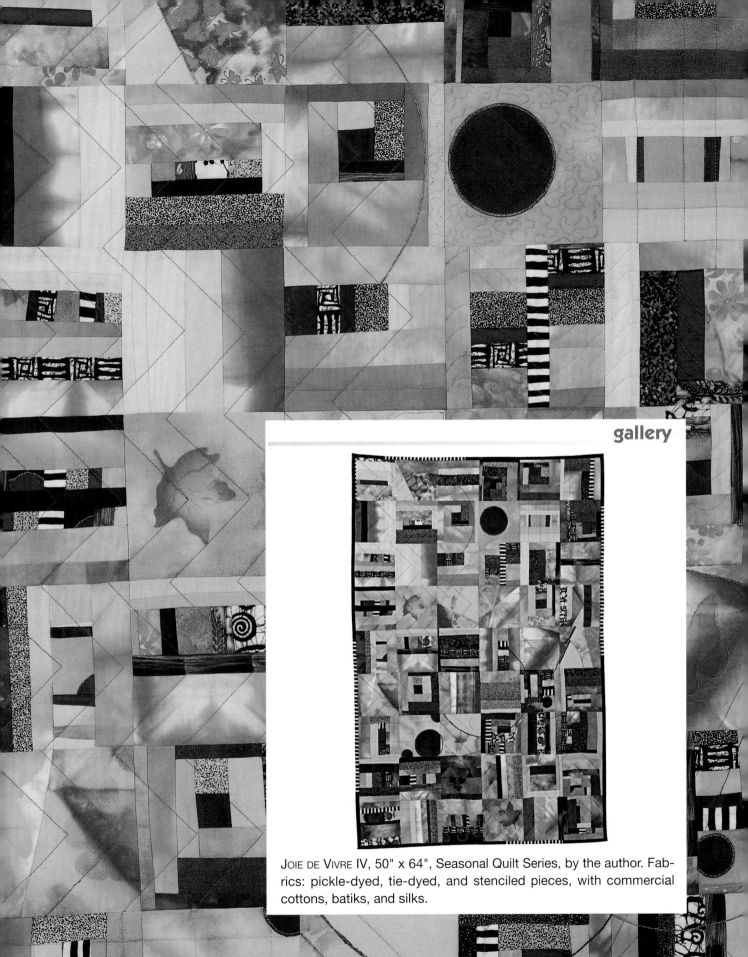

JOIE DE VIVRE IV, 50" x 64", Seasonal Quilt Series, by the author. Fabrics: pickle-dyed, tie-dyed, and stenciled pieces, with commercial cottons, batiks, and silks.

gallery

JOIE DE VIVRE V, 37" x 52", Seasonal Quilt Series, by the author. Fabrics: pickle-dyed and stenciled pieces, with commercial cottons, photographic imagery, and batiks.

RYAN'S FREEDOM, 70" x 90", by the author. This quilt was made for my son's high school graduation. Fabrics: pickle-dyed pieces with African fabrics.

GODDESS I: SARASVATI, 35" x 68", Goddess Series, by the author. In the spiritual traditions of India, Sarasvati presides over the arts, literature, and music. Fabrics: pickle-dyed, fold-dyed, tie-dyed, and stenciled pieces, with photographic imagery, paint, and silks.